Bob Lanier

THE STORY OF THE MILWAUKEE BUCKS

Khris Middleton

A HISTORY OF HOOPS

THE STORY OF THE

MILWAUKEE BUCKS

JIM WHITING

Giannis Antetokounmpo

CREATIVE EDUCATION / CREATIVE PAPERBACKS

Published by Creative Education and Creative Paperbacks
P.O. Box 227, Mankato, Minnesota 56002
Creative Education and Creative Paperbacks are imprints of
The Creative Company
www.thecreativecompany.us

Design and production by Blue Design (www.bluedes.com)
Art direction by Rita Marshall

Photographs by AP Images (Associated Press, WAS), Corbis (Steve Lipofsky),
Getty (Brian Babineau, Bettmann, Vernon Biever, Kevin C. Cox, Jonathan
Daniel, Gary Dineen, Elsa, Focus On Sport, Thearon W. Henderson, Wesley Hitt,
John Iacono, Mike McGinnis, MediaNews Group/Boston Herald, Fernando
Medina, Manny Millan, Ronald C. Modra/Sports Imagery, NBA Photo Library,
Stacy Revere), © Steve Lipofsky, Newscom (Ting Shen/Xinhua/Photoshot),
USPresswire (David Butler II)

Library of Congress Cataloging-in-Publication Data
Names: Whiting, Jim, 1943- author.
Title: The story of the Milwaukee Bucks / By Jim Whiting.
Description: Mankato, Minnesota : Creative Education and Creative
   Paperbacks, [2023] | Series: Creative Sports: A History of Hoops |
   Includes index. | Audience: Ages 8-12 |
   Audience: Grades 4-6 | Summary: "Middle grade basketball fans are
   introduced to the extraordinary history of NBA's Milwaukee Bucks with a
   photo-laden narrative of their greatest successes and losses"-- Provided
   by publisher.
Identifiers: LCCN 2022016843 (print) | LCCN 2022016844 (ebook) | ISBN
   9781640266339 (library binding) | ISBN 9781682771891 (paperback) | ISBN
   9781640007741 (pdf)
Subjects: LCSH: Milwaukee Bucks (Basketball team)--History--Juvenile
   literature. | Milwaukee Bucks (Basketball team)--Biography--Juvenile
   literatue.
Classification: LCC GV885.52.M54 W45 2023 (print) | LCC GV885.52.M54
   (ebook) | DDC 796.323/640977595--dc23
LC record available at https://lccn.loc.gov/2022016843
LC ebook record available at https://lccn.loc.gov/2022016844

Kareem Abdul Jabbar

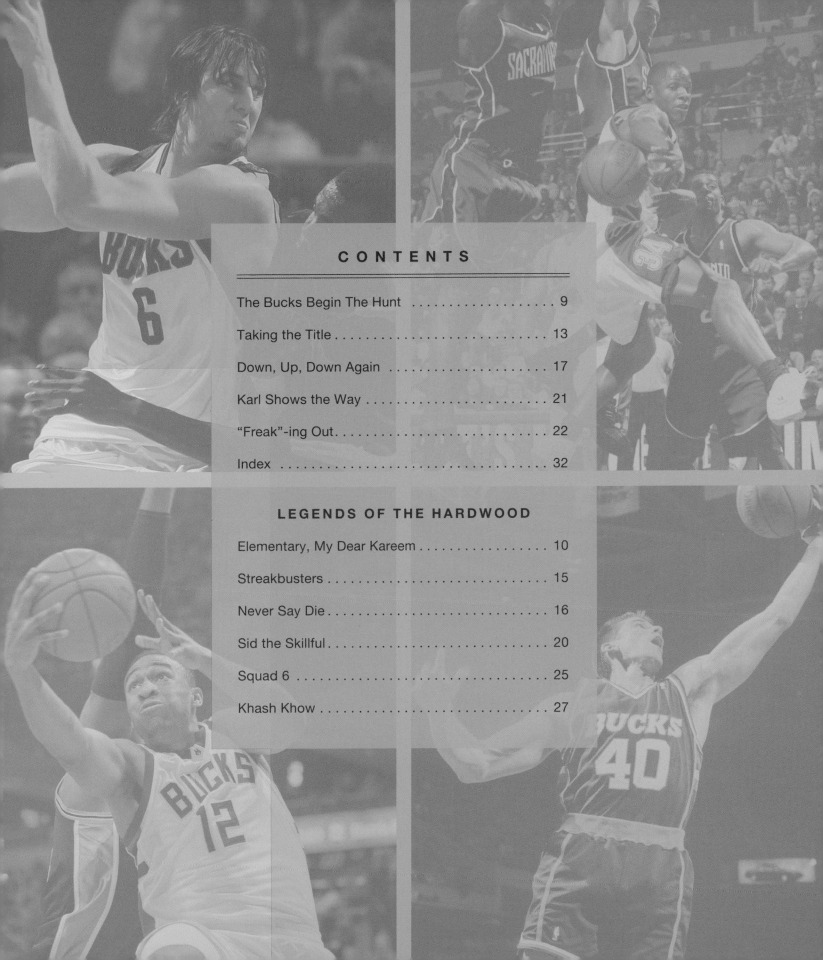

CONTENTS

LEGENDS OF THE HARDWOOD

Giannis Antetokounmpo

THE BUCKS BEGIN THE HUNT

It was the final moments of Game 7 of the 2020–21 semifinals of the National Basketball Association's (NBA) Eastern Conference. The Milwaukee Bucks led the Brooklyn Nets 109–107.

With one second remaining, Nets star forward Kevin Durant drained an apparent game-winning three-point shot. He and his teammates celebrated. The referees took a closer look. The replay showed that his foot barely touched the three-point line. The shot counted for two points, not three.

The game went to overtime. The Nets quickly scored on a putback after a missed shot. At that point the lid went onto their basket. They missed six shots in the next three minutes. Milwaukee didn't do any better. They couldn't score in four straight possessions. Their dry spell ended when do-everything star Giannis Antetokounmpo (YAA-nees aan-tuh-tuh-KOOM-po) hit a short hook shot with just over a minute left. That tied the score at 111–111.

Brooklyn missed two more shots. Milwaukee small forward Khris Middleton's 13-foot jump shot put his team ahead with 40 seconds left. Brooklyn still couldn't score. Durant missed a potential game-tying 23-foot jump shot as time ran out. Bucks center Brook Lopez was fouled. He sank two free throws. Milwaukee won 115–111. They moved on to the next round of the playoffs. They hoped to crown it with their second NBA title.

Their first one had come shortly after Milwaukee had been one of two NBA expansion teams that began playing in the 1968–69 season. The team had a contest to determine the nickname. Several suggestions were submitted. The winner was

KAREEM ABDUL-JABBAR
CENTER
HEIGHT: 7-FOOT-2
BUCKS SEASONS: 1969–75

ELEMENTARY, MY DEAR KAREEM

Since retiring, Kareem Abdul-Jabbar has become a best-selling author in several widely separated genres in both fiction and nonfiction. One is history, such as *What Color Is My World?: The Lost History of African-American Inventors*. Social issues are another. Memoirs for both adults and young readers are a third. Many educators recommend *Becoming Kareem: Growing Up On and Off the Court* to their students. The Streetball Crew series features authentic basketball action while dealing with personal issues that readers face while growing up. Adults enjoy the Mycroft and Holmes series about the famous fictional detective Sherlock Holmes, his brother Mycroft, and faithful companion Dr. John Watson.

Kareem Abdul-Jabbar

Bucks. It referred to male white-tailed deer common in Wisconsin's woods. One man who suggested the name said, "Bucks are spirited, good jumpers, fast, and agile." Those are good qualities for basketball players.

The Bucks needed all those qualities in their first season. The roster combined players other teams didn't want and raw rookies. Despite the limitations, the Bucks had a strong backcourt. Shooting guard Jon McGlocklin averaged nearly 20 points a game. Veteran point guard Guy Rodgers provided stability. He averaged 10 points and 7 assists per game.

The Bucks finished the season with 27 wins and 55 losses. It was the worst record in the NBA's Eastern Division. The Phoenix Suns had the worst record in the Western Division. Before the 1969 NBA Draft, the league conducted a coin toss between them. The winner would have the first overall pick. There was no question about that pick: seven-foot-two UCLA center Lew Alcindor. He had dominated college basketball for three years.

The coin toss took place in the league offices in New York City. Phoenix called heads. The coin came up tails. Bucks' owner Wes Pavalon was so excited that he accidentally jammed his lighted cigarette into general manager John Erickson's ear as he hugged him. "It stung a little, but I didn't notice it," Erickson said. "I didn't care, once we had Lew."

TAKING THE TITLE

Alcindor was an immediate sensation. He was unlike anyone who had ever played the game. "He may be the first of the 7-foot backcourt men," said teammate Fred Crawford. "He can dribble and make moves that no big man ever made before." He averaged nearly 29 points, 15 rebounds, and 4 assists a game. He was an obvious choice for NBA Rookie of the Year. The Bucks more than doubled their win total to 56. They beat the Philadelphia 76ers in the first round of the playoffs. But the New York Knicks knocked the Bucks out in the second round.

Milwaukee made a major addition the following year. That was point guard Oscar Robertson, nicknamed "The Big O." He had played 10 years for the Cincinnati Royals (now the Sacramento Kings) but never came close to winning an NBA title. He averaged more than 29 points and 10 assists a game during that time. In the 1961–62 season, he became just one of two players to average a triple-double for an entire season. That means he averaged double digits in points, rebounds, and assists.

The Bucks surged to 66 wins, by far the league's best record. It included winning streaks of 10, 16, and a then-NBA record 20 games. Alcindor won the NBA Most Valuable Player (MVP) award. The Bucks easily won the first two rounds of the playoffs. Then they swept the Baltimore Bullets to win the NBA championship. "We won the world championship in the Bucks' third year of existence. That's something that I'll be proud of all of my life," Alcindor said. It is the shortest

Oscar Robertson

amount of time that an expansion team had needed to take the title. Perhaps no one was happier than Robertson. It was his first NBA championship. ''The 'Big O' was usually stoic and about business and going about his task, but it was like the kid in him came out,'' said teammate Bob Dandridge.

Alcindor soon changed his name to Kareem Abdul-Jabbar. The new name reflected his Muslin faith. The Bucks continued to play at a high level for the next three years. Abdul-Jabbar was named MVP two more times. But Milwaukee couldn't win another title. They came close in 1974. They played the Boston Celtics in the Finals. Boston won, 4 games to 3. Robertson retired. Milwaukee struggled to a 38–44 mark. When the Bucks drafted Abdul-Jabbar, he had said, ''I was disappointed that I couldn't go play where I wanted to play—either in New York or San Francisco or Los Angeles.'' Now he felt it was time to leave Milwaukee. He asked team officials to trade him to the Los Angeles Lakers.

Lucius Allen

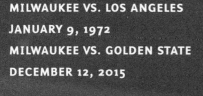

MILWAUKEE VS. LOS ANGELES
JANUARY 9, 1972
MILWAUKEE VS. GOLDEN STATE
DECEMBER 12, 2015

LEGENDS
OF THE HARDWOOD

STREAKBUSTERS

Led by massive center Wilt Chamberlain and All-Star guard Jerry West, the Lakers ran off 33 wins in a row during the 1971–72 season. It remains the longest streak in NBA history. Abdul-Jabbar led the way as the Bucks ended it with a 120–104 win. He scored 39 points and hauled down 20 rebounds. Ironically, he would become a Laker four seasons later. The Warriors had an NBA-record 24 wins to start the 2015–16 season. Once again it was the Bucks who played spoilers. Supported by hundreds of fans wearing pregame-printed "24–1" T-shirts, Milwaukee won 108–95. The streak-stopper was actually a two-for-one. Golden State had won the final four games the previous season. The overlapping 28-game winning streak was the second-longest in league history.

MILWAUKEE BUCKS

Marques Johnson

LEGENDS OF THE HARDWOOD

NEVER SAY DIE

MILWAUKEE VS. ATLANTA, NOVEMBER 25, 1977

The Bucks weren't having a good night. With 8:43 left in the game, they trailed the Hawks by 29 points. The score was 111–82. Making things more difficult, they were playing on the road. At that time, there were no three-point shots. So it was even harder to claw back from such a deep deficit. Yet from that point on, the Bucks scored 35 points. Their stifling defense limited Atlanta to just *four* points. Small forward Marques Johnson sank two free throws in the final second for the 117–115 win. It is the greatest fourth-quarter comeback in NBA history.

DOWN, UP, DOWN AGAIN

ilwaukee struggled for the next four seasons. They had just one winning record. Things changed in the 1979–80 season. Milwaukee obtained massive 6-foot-10 center Bob Lanier in a midseason trade. He joined rookie guard Sidney Moncrief. They helped the team return to the winning column with 49 victories. The Bucks won a whopping 60 games in 1980–81 and followed up with 55 wins the next season. But each time they fell in the conference semifinals.

The Bucks advanced to the Eastern Conference finals in both 1983 and 1984. They lost both times. Lanier retired. The team responded by winning 59 games in 1984–85. They won 57 and 50 the next two seasons. Each time they won in the first round of the playoffs, advancing to the conference finals in 1985–86. But returning to the championship series proved elusive.

A disappointed Moncrief left Milwaukee after the 1988–89 season. "It's a shame we never won a championship with those teams," he said. "We always had championship heart." The team's victory totals fell off slightly the next two years. They still made the playoffs. But the pattern of early elimination continued.

The wheels started coming off in the 1991–92 season. The team went 31–51. It was the first time the Bucks had missed the playoffs in 13 years. The team had losing records for the next seven seasons. The low point came in 1993–94. Milwaukee won only 20 games. That was the lowest win total in franchise history up to that point.

Glenn Robinson

A bright spot was rookie center/power forward Vin Baker, who averaged nearly 14 points and 8 rebounds a game. Milwaukee drafted well again the following year. They took National College Player of the Year Glenn "Big Dog" Robinson. Team officials and fans were especially delighted when Robinson led all rookies in scoring with an average of nearly 22 points a game.

Robinson and Baker helped Milwaukee improve to 34 wins in 1994–95. But the Bucks fell back to 25–57 in the following season. Immediately after the 1996 Draft, the Bucks traded for slick-shooting rookie guard Ray Allen. His three-pointers were especially deadly. "You think you're doing pretty well against this kid, and then you look up, and he's got 20 points," said Minnesota Timberwolves guard Doug West. Despite all these additions, though, the Bucks posted losing records in the next two seasons.

Vin Baker

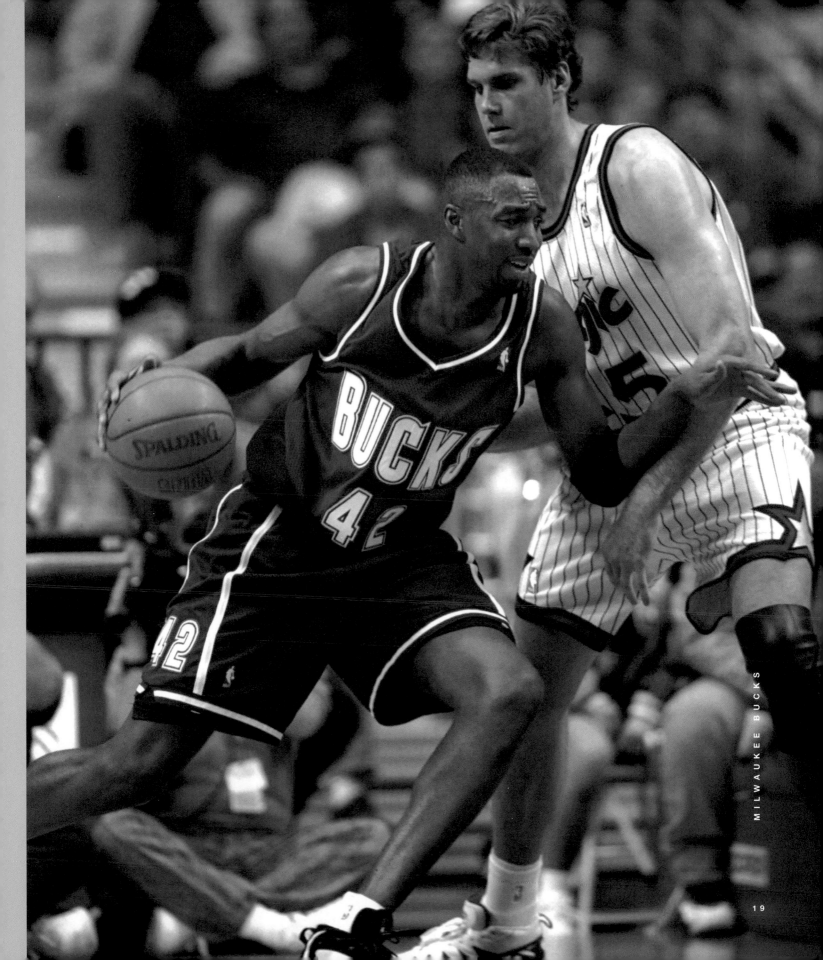

SIDNEY MONCRIEF
POINT/SHOOTING GUARD
HEIGHT: 6-FOOT-3
BUCKS SEASONS: 1979–89

SID THE SKILLFUL

Sidney Moncrief was one of the most versatile players during the 1980s. As NBA writer Steve Aschburner notes, "He attacked the basket on drives and with post-up moves, developed an outside shot on the fly, perpetually moved both himself and the ball, and dared to crash the boards when dinosaurs [big men with limited mobility] still ruled the NBA paint." Moncrief averaged 20 points a game for five straight seasons. He was even better on defense. The NBA established the Defensive Player of the Year award in 1982. Moncrief was the first winner. And the next. He was nicknamed "Sir Sid" because of the respect he commanded throughout the league. He credited his mom for his development. "She always took the time for discipline," Moncrief said. "I had to do things right. It gave me a very strong foundation to work from."

KARL SHOWS THE WAY

After the 1997–98 season, the team hired George Karl as coach. In Seattle, his teams won at least 55 games seven seasons in a row. "This team has talent," Karl said, "but they need to play together and learn defensive discipline." His first season was shortened due to a conflict between owners and players. It lasted for several months. The Bucks went 28–22. They returned to the playoffs, though the Indiana Pacers swept them in the first round.

Milwaukee added point guard Sam Cassell for veteran leadership. Along with Robinson and Allen, Cassell formed Milwaukee's "Big Three." The Bucks faced the Pacers again in the first round of the 2000 playoffs. They lost the series-deciding game by a single point. "We played them tough," Robinson said. "But a loss like this makes us realize we can do great things."

It seemed like Milwaukee would do great things in 2000–01. The Bucks won 52 games. It was their highest win total in 15 years. They won the first two rounds of the playoffs. They faced the 76ers in the Eastern Conference finals. They split the first four games. The Bucks lost Game 5 in heartbreaking fashion, 89-88. Robinson missed a short jumper in the final seconds. Allen couldn't tip in the rebound. The Bucks tied the series in the next game as Allen poured in 41 points. But he was injured in the deciding Game 7. Philadelphia's Allen Iverson torched the Bucks for 44 points. The Sixers won easily, 108–91.

That series was the high-water mark for the Bucks between the 2001–02 and 2012–13 seasons. Win totals ranged from 28 (2007–08) to 46 (2009–10). Their five playoff appearances all ended with first-round defeats.

Help was on the way. It couldn't have come from a more unlikely source.

"FREAK"-ING OUT

Charles and Veronica Antetokounmpo had come to Athens, Greece from their native Nigeria in 1991. They eventually had four sons. The family's life was hard. They faced racial discrimination. Money was always an issue. Few people would hire them because they were black. The two oldest boys, Thanasis and Giannis, spent endless hours selling trinkets on the streets. Sometimes the family was evicted from its cramped apartments because they couldn't pay the rent. They often went to bed hungry.

Giannis began playing basketball when he was 13. He spent hour after hour on the court. He was rail-thin due to lack of food. Opponents pushed him around. Slowly he improved. So did his reputation. Swarms of NBA personnel began packing the tiny gyms where he was playing. But his games were far from NBA-caliber. It seemed obvious that he would need several years to develop.

The Bucks drafted Antetokounmpo in 2013 when he was still 18. Almost no one realized it at the time, but the Bucks' long hunt for a difference maker was about

Giannis Antetokounmpo

ANDREW BOGUT
CENTER
HEIGHT: 7-FOOT-0
BUCKS SEASONS: 2005–12

SQUAD 6

Andrew Bogut was the first overall choice in the 2005 NBA Draft. He wanted to add noise and excitement to home games. "A lot of times it was very, very quiet," he said. In 2009, Bogut formed Squad 6. He bought 100 seats for every game. He held auditions to see who was loudest and rowdiest. The winners got free tickets. Six was Bogut's jersey number. It also stood for the "sixth man," who supported the five players on the court. "It's only 100 people," Bogut said, "but the noise they make sounds like 1,000. It gives us some energy to feed off." Some opponents also liked Squad 6. "Those fans were the most fun fans I have seen on the road EVER," said Dallas Mavericks owner Mark Cuban. Today it is called the Clutch Crew. Its sponsor is the Harley-Davidson Motorcycle Company, headquartered in Milwaukee.

MILWAUKEE BUCKS

to end. Antetokounmpo became known as "the Greek Freak." He was a "freak of nature," able to play every position except center. It took him time to adjust to the NBA. The team suffered through a franchise-worst 15–67 mark in his rookie year.

Three years later, Antetokounmpo was named NBA Most Improved Player. Shooting/point guard Malcolm Brogdon was NBA Rookie of the Year. Milwaukee went 42–40. It was Milwaukee's first winning record in seven seasons. They improved to 44–38 the following season. In both seasons they lost in the first round of the playoffs.

Antetokounmpo improved even more in 2018–19. He became just the third player in NBA history with averages of at least 25 points, 10 rebounds, 5 assists, 1 blocked shot, and 1 steal per game during an entire season. Only NBA legends Larry Bird and Kareem Abdul-Jabbar accomplished the same thing. He was named NBA MVP as Milwaukee surged to a 60–22 mark. They reached the Eastern Conference finals but lost to the Toronto Raptors, 4 games to 2. Antetokounmpo was both NBA MVP and NBA Defensive Player of the Year the following season, though Milwaukee fell to the Miami Heat in the second round of the playoffs.

The Bucks wanted to do something special in 2020–21. It was the 50th anniversary of their first (and only) NBA title. They swept Miami in the first round. After the dramatic victory over the Nets, they took down the Atlanta Hawks in the conference finals. They faced the Phoenix Suns for the NBA championship. Phoenix won the first two games. Milwaukee took the next two. The Bucks eked out a 4-point win in Game 5. Antetokounmpo scored 50 points, pulled down 14 rebounds, and blocked 5 shots as the Bucks closed out the series in Game 6,

KHRIS MIDDLETON
SMALL FORWARD
HEIGHT: 6-FOOT-7
BUCKS SEASONS: 2013-PRESENT

KHASH KHOW

The Detroit Pistons didn't think very highly of Khris Middleton when they drafted him in 2012. He averaged just six points a game as a rookie. After the season, he was a throw-in in a trade that sent him to Milwaukee. He flowered with the Bucks. In the past few years, he is often the player the team turns to when they need a "money shot," a basket that determines the outcome of a game. "Milwaukee putting trust in Middleton to carry them home late has been a natural progression all season long, both in the regular season and now in the playoffs," wrote Jordan Treske of Fanside during the 2021 NBA Finals. And according to ESPN, Middleton and LeBron James have had the most game-tying or go-ahead baskets in a single playoff run in the last 25 years.

Jrue Holiday

105–98. He became just the seventh player to score 50 or more points in a Finals game. He celebrated by ordering 50 chicken nuggets at a fast-food restaurant. "This was my city," he said. "So many people believed in me and helped me get to this point."

The Bucks finished the 2021–22 season with a 51–31 record. Antetokounmpo averaged a career-high 29.9 points per game. Milwaukee faced the Chicago Bulls in the first round of the playoffs. The teams split the first two games. The Bucks won the next three by an average of more than 23 points per game.

Milwaukee took on the Boston Celtics in the conference semifinals. They played it without Khris Middleton had been injured in the Chicago series. Still, Milwaukee won the first, third, and fifth games. Boston won the second, fourth, and sixth. In Game 7, the Bucks jumped out to an early 10-point lead. Boston came back to lead by five points at halftime. The Celtics dominated the second half. They outscored Milwaukee 61–38 to win, 109–81. The Bucks were a horrendous 4-for-33 in three-point attempts. On the other hand, Antetokounmpo became the first player with 200 points, 100 rebounds, and 50 assists in a single playoff series. "I wish we were the team that would play on Tuesday [in the conference finals], but we're not," he said. "At the end of the day, when somebody beats you, you've got to respect it."

The Bucks got off to the best start in NBA history by going from expansion team to league champions in just three seasons. Then they were golden on their golden (50th) anniversary. Fans hope that the team's young talent will result in more championship banners in the coming years.

Giannis Antetokounmpo passes to Grayson Allen

INDEX